MW01201781

POWER AND USE OF THOUGHT

CHARLES LEADBEATER

POWER AND USE OF THOUGHT

THOSE who are ignorant of Theosophy sometimes suppose it to be merely a system of speculative philosophy. Nothing could be farther from the truth than this; there is nothing in any way speculative about it, for it is founded entirely upon observation of facts, and upon experiments made in connection with the phenomena and the forces of Nature. From its study emerges a practical rule of life — a rule which cannot but affect the thought and action of its students at every moment of their existence. This is chiefly because it involves a study of life as it really is, so that its students become acquainted with the whole of the world in which they live, instead of knowing only the least important part of it. They are led to understand the laws of evolution; and they naturally learn to live intelligently in accordance with those laws, and to take into account the unseen part of the world as well as the infinitesimal portion which is within reach of the limited physical senses.

Of the general nature of the unseen world I have written elsewhere. For the moment, let us concentrate our attention on one of its most striking characteristics — the ready response of the finer types of matter (of which it is constructed) to the influences of human thought and emotion. It is difficult for those who have not studied the subject to grasp the absolute reality of these forces — to understand that they are in every respect as definite in their action upon the finer type of matter as is the power of steam or electricity over physical matter. Every one knows that a man who has at his disposal a large amount of steam power or electrical power can do useful work and produce definite results; but few people know that every man has at his disposal a certain amount of this other and higher power, and that with that he can produce results just as definite and just as real. As matters stand at present in the physical world, only a few men can have at their disposal any large amount of its forces, and so only a few can become rich by their means; but it is a prominent feature of the vivid interest of the unseen side of life, that every human being, rich or poor, old or young, has already at his disposal no inconsiderable proportion of its forces. And therefore the riches of these higher planes, which are obtained by the right use of these powers, are within the reach of all.

Here, then, is a power possessed by all, but intelligently used as yet by few. It is, surely well worth our while to take up the matter, to enquire into it, and to try to comprehend it.

Indeed there is even more reason for so doing than has yet been mentioned; for the truth is that to some extent we are all already unconsciously making use of this power, and because of our ignorance we are employing it wrongly, and doing harm with it instead of good. The possession of power always means responsibility; so in order to avoid doing harm unintentionally, and in order to utilize thoroughly these magnificent possibilities, it will clearly be well for us to learn all that we can on this subject.

What, then, is THOUGHT, and how does it show itself ? Those who have even a superficial acquaintance with Theosophical literature are aware that man possesses a vehicle corresponding to each of the interpenetrating worlds of our solar system — that his astral body is the vehicle of his desires, passions, and emotions; and that his thought expresses itself through that higher vehicle of still finer matter which we usually call the mental body. It is in this latter vehicle that thought first shows itself to the sight of the clairvoyant; and it appears as a vibration of its matter — a vibration which is found to produce various effects, all of them quite in line with what scientific experience in the physical world would lead us to expect.

First there is the effect produced

upon the mental body itself; and we find that to be of the nature of setting up a habit. There are many different types of matter in the mental body, and each of them appears to have its own special rate of oscillation, to which it seems most accustomed, so that it readily responds to it and tends to return thereto as soon as possible when it has been forced away from it by some strong rush of thought or feeling. A sufficiently strong thought may for the moment set the whole of the matter of the mental body swinging at the same rate; and every time that that happens it is a little easier for it to happen again. A habit of vibrating at that rate is being set up in the mental body, so that the man will readily repeat that particular thought.

Secondly, there is the effect produced upon the other vehicles of the man, which are above and below the mental body in degree of density. We know that in the physical world disturbances in one type of matter are readily communicated to another type — that, for example, an earthquake will produce a mighty wave in the sea and again (from the other side) that the disturbance of the air by a storm will immediately produce ripples, and presently great waves, in the ocean beneath it. In just the same way a disturbance in a man's astral body (that is to say, what we commonly call an emotion) will set up undulations in the mental body, and cause thoughts which correspond to the emotion. Conversely, the movement in the mental body affects the astral body, if it be of a type which can affect it — which means that certain types of thought will readily provoke emotion. Just as the mental vibration acts upon the astral matter, which is denser than it is, so also does it inevitably act upon the matter of the causal body, which is finer than it. Thus the habitual thought of the man builds up qualities in the ego himself.

So far, we have been dealing with the effect of the man's thought upon himself; and we see that in the first place it tends to repeat itself, and that in the second place it acts not only upon his emotions, but also permanently upon the man himself. Now let us turn to the effects which it produces outside of himself — that is, upon the sea of mental matter which surrounds us all, just as does the atmosphere.

Thirdly, then, every thought produces a radiating undulation, which may be either simple or complex according to the nature of the thought that gives it birth. This vibration may under certain conditions be confined to the mental world, but also it may produce an effect in worlds above and below. If the thought be purely intellectual and impersonal — if, for example, the thinker is considering a philosophical system, or attempting to solve a problem in algebra or geometry — the wave sent forth will affect merely the mental matter. If the thought be of a spiritual nature, if it be tinged with love or aspiration, or with deep unselfish feeling, it will rise upwards into the realm of the higher mental, and may even borrow some of the splendour and glory of the intuitional level — a combination which renders it exceedingly powerful. If, on the other hand, the thought is tinged with something of self or of personal desire, its oscillations at once draw downwards and expend most of their force in the astral world.

All these undulations act upon their respective levels just as does a vibration of light or sound here in the physical world. They radiate out in all directions, becoming less powerful in proportion to their distance from their source. But we should remember that the radiations affect not only the sea of mental matter which surrounds us, but also act upon other mental bodies moving within that sea. We are all familiar with the experiment in which a note struck on a piano, or a string sounded on a violin, will set the corresponding note sounding upon another instrument of the same kind, which has been tuned exactly to the same pitch. Just as the vibration set up in one instrument is conveyed through the air and acts upon the other instrument, so is the thought-vibration set up in one mental body conveyed by the surrounding mental matter and reproduced in another mental body — which, stated from another point of view, means that thought is infectious. We will return to this consideration later.

Fourthly, every thought produces not only an undulation but a form — a definite, separate object, which is endowed with force and vitality of a certain kind, and in many cases behaves like a temporary living creature. This form, like the vibration, may be in the mental world only; but much more frequently it descends to the astral level and produces its principal effect in the world of emotions. The study of these thought-forms is of exceeding interest; a detailed account of many of them, with coloured illustrations of their appearance, will be found in a book called *Thought-Forms*, which can be had at *The Theosophist Office*. At the moment, we are concerned less with their appearance than with their effects and with the way in which they can be utilized.

Let us consider separately the action of these two manifestations of thought-power. The vibration may be simple or it may be complex, according to the character of the thought; but its strength is poured out chiefly upon some one of the four levels of mental matter — the four subdivisions which constitute the lower part of the mental world. Most of the thoughts of the ordinary man center round himself, his desires, and his emotions, and they are therefore undulations of the lowest subdivision of mental matter; indeed, the corresponding part of the mental body is the only one which is as yet fully developed and active in the great majority of mankind. It must not be forgotten that in this respect the condition of the mental body is very different from that of the astral vehicle. In the ordinary cultured man of our race the astral body is, as fully developed as the physical, and the man is perfectly capable of using it as a vehicle of consciousness. He is not yet much in the habit of so using it, and is consequently shy about it and distrustful of his powers; but the astral powers are all there, and it is simply a question of becoming accustomed to their use. When he finds himself functioning in the astral world either during sleep or after death, he is fully capable of sight and hearing, and can move about whithersoever he will.

In the heaven-world, however, he finds himself under very different conditions, for the mental body is as yet by no means fully developed, that being the part of its evolution upon which the human race is at the present moment engaged. The mental body can be employed as a vehicle only by those who have been specially trained in its use under

Teachers belonging to the Great Brotherhood of Initiates; in the average man it is only partially developed, and cannot in the least be employed as a separate vehicle of consciousness. In the majority of men the higher portions of the mental body are as yet quite dormant, even when, the lower portions are in vigorous activity. This necessarily implies that while the whole mental atmosphere is surging with vibrations belonging to the lowest subdivision, there is as yet comparatively little activity on the higher subdivisions — a fact which we shall need to have clearly in mind when we come to consider presently the practical possibility of the use of thought-power. It has also an important bearing upon the distance to which a thought-wave may penetrate.

The distance covered by such a wave, and the strength and persistence with which it can impinge upon the mental bodies of others, depend upon the strength and clearness of the original thought. In this respect it resembles the voice of a speaker, setting in motion waves of sound in the air, which radiate from him in all directions, and convey his words to all those who are (as we say) within hearing; and the distance to which his voice can penetrate depends upon its strength and the clearness of his enunciation. In exactly the same way a strong thought will carry much farther than one which is weak and undecided; but clearness and distinctness are of even greater importance than strength. Again, just as the speaker's voice may fall upon heedless ears where men are already engaged in business or in pleasure, so may a strong wave of thought sweep past without affecting the mind of a man if he is already wholly engrossed in some other line of thought. Many men, however, do not think definitely or strongly except when in the immediate prosecution of some business that demands their whole attention, so that there are always within reach many minds that are liable to be considerably affected by the thoughts which impinge upon them.

The action of this undulation is eminently adaptable. It may exactly reproduce itself, if it finds a mental body which readily responds to it in every particular; but when this is not the case, it may nevertheless produce a decided effect along lines broadly similar to its own. Suppose for example, that a Catholic kneels in devotion before an image of the Blessed Virgin. He sends rippling out from him in all directions strong devotional vibrations; if they strike upon the mental or astral body of another Catholic, they will arouse in him a thought and feeling identical with the original. But if they should strike upon a Christian of some other sect, to whom the image of the Blessed Virgin is unfamiliar, they will still awaken in him the sentiment of devotion, but that will follow along its accustomed channel, and be directed towards the Christ.

In the same way, if they should touch a Muhammadan they would arouse in him devotion to Allah, while in the case of a Hindû the object might be Krshna, and in the case of a Pãrsî, Ahuramazda. But they would excite devotion of some sort wherever there was a possibility of response to that idea. If, however, they should touch the mental body of a materialist, to whom the very idea of devotion in any form is unknown, they would still produce an elevating effect. They could not at once create a type of vibration to which the man was wholly unaccustomed, but their tendency would be to stir a higher part of his mental body into some sort of activity; and the effect, though less permanent than in the case of the sympathetic recipient, could not fail to be good.

The action of an evil or impure thought is governed by the same laws. A man who is so foolish as to allow himself to think of another with hatred or envy radiates a wave tending to provoke similar passions in others; and though his feeling of hatred be for someone quite unknown to these others, and so it is impossible that they should share it, yet the radiation will stir in them an emotion of the same nature towards a totally different person.

The work of the thought-form is more limited, but much more precise than that of the undulation. It cannot reach so many persons — indeed we may say that it cannot act upon a person at all unless he has in him something which is harmonious with the vibrant energy which ensouls it. The powers and possibilities of these thought-forms will perhaps be clearer to us if we attempt to classify them. Let us consider first the thought which is definitely directed towards another person — as when a man sends forth from himself a thought of affection or of gratitude (or unfortunately it may be sometimes of envy or jealousy) towards someone else. Such a thought will produce radiating waves precisely as would any other, and will therefore tend to reproduce itself in the minds of those within the sphere of its influence. But the thought-form which it creates is imbued with definite intention, as it were; and as soon as it breaks away from the mental and astral bodies of the thinkers it goes straight towards the person to whom it is directed, and fastens itself upon him.

It may be compared not inaptly to a Leyden jar with its charge of electricity — the matter of the mental and astral worlds forming the body, which is symbolized by the jar, and the vibrant energy of the thought which ensouls it corresponding to the charge of electricity. If the man towards whom it is directed is at the moment in a passive condition, or if he has within him active oscillations of a character harmonious with its own, it will at once discharge itself upon him. Its effect will naturally be to provoke an undulation similar to its own if none such previously existed, and to intensify it if it is already to be found there. If the man's mind is for the time so strongly occupied along some other lines that it is impossible for the vibration to find an entrance, the thought-form hovers about him waiting for an opportunity to discharge itself.

In the case of a thought which is not

directed to some other person, but is connected chiefly with the thinker himself (as indeed are the majority of man's thoughts), the undulation spreads in all directions as usual, but the thought-form floats in the immediate neighbourhood of its creator, and its tendency is constantly to react upon him. As long as his mind is fully occupied with business, or with a thought of some other type, the floating form simply bides its time; but when his train of thought is exhausted, or his mind for a moment lies fallow, it has an opportunity to react upon him, and immediately it begins to repeat itself — to stir up in his mind a repetition of the thought to which he has previously yielded himself. Many a man may be seen surrounded by a shell of such thought-forms, and he will frequently feel their pressure upon him — a constant suggestion from without of certain thoughts; and if the thought be evil, he very likely believes himself to be tempted by the devil: whereas the truth is that he is his own tempter, and that the evil thoughts are entirely his own creation.

Thirdly, there is the class of thought which is neither centered round the thinker nor aimed specially at any person. The thought-form generated in this case does not hang about the thinker, nor has it any special attraction towards another man, so it simply remains idly floating where it was called into existence. Each man as he moves through life is thus producing three classes of thought-forms — those which shoot straight out away from him, aiming at a definite objective; those which hover round him and follow him wherever he goes; and those which he leaves behind him as a sort of trail which marks his route.

The whole atmosphere is filled with thought of this third type, vague and indeterminate; so that as we walk along we are, as it were, picking our way through vast masses of them; and if our minds are not already definitely occupied, these vague wandering fragments of other people's thought will seriously affect us. They, sweep through the mind which is lying idle, and probably the majority of them do not arouse in it any especial interest; but now and then comes one which attracts attention, and the mind fastens upon it, entertains it for a moment or two, and dismisses it a little stronger than it was on arrival. Naturally this mixture of thought from many sources has no definite coherence — though it must be remembered that any one of these may start a line of associated ideas, and so set the mind thinking on its own account. If a man pulls himself up suddenly as he walks along the street, and asks himself: " What am I thinking about, and why ? How did I reach this particular point in my train of thought ?" and if he tries to follow back the line of his thoughts for the last ten minutes, he will probably be quite surprised to discover how many idle and useless thoughts have passed through his mind in that space of time. They are not one-fourth of them his own thoughts; they are simply those fragments which he has picked up as he passed along. In most cases they are quite valueless, and their general tendency is distinctly more likely to be evil than good.

Now that we understand to some extent the action of thought, let us see what use it is possible to make of this knowledge, and what practical considerations emerge from it. Knowing these things, what can we do to forward our own evolution, and what can we do to help others ? Obviously, a scientific consideration of the way in which thought works exhibits it as a matter of far greater importance for evolution than we ordinarily suppose. Since every thought or emotion produces a permanent effect by strengthening or weakening a tendency, and since, furthermore, every thought-vibration and thought-form must inevitably react upon the thinker, the greatest care must be exercised as to the thought or emotion which the man permits within himself. The ordinary man rarely thinks of attempting to check an emotion; when he feels it surging within him he yields himself to it and considers it merely natural.

One who studies scientifically the action of these forces realizes that it is his interest as well as his duty to check every such upwelling, and consider before he allows it to sway him whether it is or is not prejudicial to his evolution.

Instead of allowing his emotions to run away with him he must have them absolutely under control; and since the stage of evolution at which we have arrived is the development of the mental body, he must take this matter also seriously in hand and see what can be done to assist that development. Instead of allowing the mind to indulge in its vagaries he should endeavour to assert control over it, recognizing that the mind is not the man, but is an instrument which the man must learn to use. It must not be left to lie fallow; it must not be allowed to remain idle, so that any passing thought-form can drift in upon it and impress it. The worthy Dr. Watts long ago remarked that " Satan finds some mischief still for idle hands to do," and certainly there is truth in the saying when it is applied to these higher levels, for the mind which is left unoccupied is far more likely to take up evil impressions than good ones. The first step towards control of the mind is to learn to keep it usefully occupied — to have some definite good and useful set of thoughts as a background to the mind's operation — something upon which it shall always fall back when there is no immediate need for its activity in connection with duty to be done.

Another most necessary point in its training is that it shall be taught to do thoroughly that which it has to do — in other words, that the power of concentration shall be acquired. This is no light task, as any unpracticed person will find who endeavours to keep his mind absolutely upon one point even for five minutes. He will find that there is an active tendency to wander — that all kinds of other thoughts thrust themselves in; the first effort to fix the mind on one subject, for five minutes is likely to resolve itself into spending five minutes in bringing the mind back again and again from various side-issues which it has followed. Fortunately, though concentration itself is no easy thing, there are plenty of opportunities for attempting it, and the acquisition of it will be of great use in our daily life. We should learn then, whatever we are doing, to focus our attention upon it, and to do it with all our might and as well as it can be done; if we write a letter, let that letter be well and accurately written, and let no carelessness in detail delay it or mar its effect; if we are reading a book, even though it be only a novel, let us read it with attention, trying to grasp the author's meaning, and to gain from it all that there is to be gained. The endeavour to be constantly learning something, to let no day pass without some definite exercise of the mind, is a most salutary one; for it is only by exercise that strength comes, and thus disuse means always weakness and eventual atrophy.

Another point of great importance is that we should learn to husband our energy. Each man possesses only a certain amount of energy, and he is responsible for its utilization to the best advantage. The ordinary man wastes his force in the most foolish manner; but it is especially necessary for the student of occultism to learn to avoid this. The average man is simply a center of agitated vibration; he is constantly in a condition of worry, of trouble about something, or in a condition of deep depression, or else he is unduly excited in the endeavour to grasp something. For one reason or another he is always in a state of unnecessary agitation, usually about the merest trifle. Although he never thinks about it, he is all the while influencing other people around him by this condition of his astral and mental bodies; he is constantly communicating these vibrations and this agitation to those unfortunate people who are near him. It is just because millions of people are thus unnecessarily agitated by all sorts of foolish desires and feelings that it is difficult for a sensitive person to live in a large city, or to go into a great crowd of his fellow-men.

Another way in which the average man wastes a great deal of force is by unnecessary argument. It appears to be impossible for him to hold any opinion, whether it be religious or political, or relating to some matter in ordinary life, without becoming a prey to an overmastering desire to force this opinion upon everyone else. He seems quite incapable of grasping the rudimentary fact that what another man chooses to believe is no business of his, and that he is not commissioned by the authorities in charge of the world to go round and secure uniformity in thought and practice. The wise man realizes that truth is a many-sided thing, not commonly held in its entirety by any one man, or by any one set of men; he knows that there is room for diversity of opinion upon almost any conceivable subject, and that therefore a man whose point of view is opposite to his own may nevertheless have something of reason and truth in his belief, He knows that most of the subjects over which men argue are not in the least worth the trouble of discussion, and that those who speak most loudly and most confidently about them are usually those who know least. The student of occultism will therefore decline to waste his time in argument; if he is asked for information he is quite willing to give it, but not to waste his time and strength in unprofitable wrangling.

Another painfully common method of wasting strength is in worry. Many men are constantly forecasting evil for themselves and for those whom they love — troubling themselves with the fear of death and of what comes after it, with the fear of financial ruin or loss of social position. A vast amount of strength is frittered away along these unprofitable and unpleasant lines; but all such foolishness is swept aside for the man who realizes that the world is governed by a law of absolute justice, that progress towards the highest is the Divine Will for him, that he cannot escape from that progress, that whatever comes in his way and whatever happens to him is meant to help him along that line, and that he himself is the only person who can delay that advance. He no longer troubles and fears about himself and about others; he simply goes on and does the duty that comes nearest in the best way that, he can, confident that if he does that, all will be well for him. He knows that worry never yet helped anyone, nor has it ever been of the slightest use, but that it has been responsible for an immense amount of evil and waste of force.

The wise man declines to spend his strength in ill-directed emotion. For example, he will utterly decline to take offence at what is said or done by someone else. If another man says something which is untrue or offensive, it is certain that in nine cases out of ten there was no evil intention behind the remark, so that it is not only foolish but unjust to be disturbed about it. Even in the rare case where the remark is intentionally wicked and spiteful — where the man said something purposely to wound another — it is still utterly foolish for that other to allow himself to feel hurt. The irritating word does not in any way injure him, except in so far as he may choose to take it up and injure himself by brooding over it or allowing himself to be wounded in his feelings. What are the words of another, that he should let his serenity be disturbed by them ? If he permits himself to care about what another, has said, then it is he himself who is responsible for the disturbance created in his mental body, and not the other man. The other has done and can do nothing that can harm him, and if the student feels hurt and injured, and thereby makes a great deal of trouble for himself, he has only himself to thank for it. If he suffers a disturbance to arise within his mental body or his astral body in reference to something that another has said, that is merely because he has not yet perfect control over his vehicles; he has not yet developed the common-sense which enables him to look down as a soul upon all this, and to go on his way and attend to his own work without taking the slightest notice of foolish or spiteful remarks made by others.

But this is after all only one side of the matter, and that the least important. It is certainly necessary for his own evolution that man should keep mind and emotion under control, and not foolishly waste his force; but it is assuredly still more necessary from another point of view, because it is only by such care that he can enable himself to be of use to his fellow-men, that he can avoid doing harm to them and can learn how to do good. If, for example, he lets himself feel angry, he naturally produces a serious effect upon himself, because he sets up an evil habit and makes it more difficult to resist the evil impulse next time it assails him. But he also acts seriously upon others around him, for inevitably the vibration which radiates from him must affect them also. If he is making an effort to control his irritability, so perhaps are they, and his action will help or hinder them, even though he is not in the least thinking of them. Every time that he allows himself to send out a wave of anger, that tends to arouse a similar vibration in the mind or astral body of another — to arouse it if it has not previously existed, and to intensify it if it is already present; and thus he makes his brother's work of self-development harder for him, and places a heavier burden upon his shoulders. On the other hand, if he controls and represses that wave of anger, lie radiates instead calming and soothing influences which are distinctly helpful to all those near him who are engaged in the same struggle.

Inevitably and without any effort of ours any thought which arises within our minds must be influencing the minds of others about us. Consider then the responsibility if a thought be impure or evil, for we are then spreading moral contagion among our fellow-men. Hundreds and thousands of people possess within them latent germs of evil — germs which may never blossom and bear fruit unless some force from without plays upon them and stirs them into activity. If we yield ourselves to an impure or unholy thought, the wave of force which we thus produce may be the very factor which awakens the germ and causes it to begin to grow, and so we may start some soul upon a downward career. The impulse so given may blossom out later into thoughts and words and deeds of evil, and these in their turn may injuriously affect thousands of other men even in the far distant future. We see then how terrible is the responsibility of a single impure or evil thought. Happily all this is true of good thought as well as of evil, and the man who realizes this may set himself to work to be a veritable sun, constantly radiating upon all his neighbours thoughts of love and calm and peace. This is a truly magnificent power, yet it is within the reach of every human being, of the poorest as well as the wealthiest, of the little child as well as the great sage.

Possessing this tremendous power, we must be careful how we exercise it. We must remember to think of a person as we wish him to be, for the image that we thus make of him will naturally act powerfully upon him and tend to draw him gradually into harmony with itself. Let us fix our thoughts upon the good qualities of our friends, because in thinking of any quality we tend to strengthen its undulations, and therefore to intensify it.

From this consideration it follows that the habit of gossip and scandal, in which many people thoughtlessly indulge themselves, is in reality a horrible wickedness, in condemning which no expression can be too strong. When people are guilty of the impertinence of discussing others, it is not usually upon the good qualities that they most insist. We have therefore a number of people fixing their thought upon some alleged evil in another, calling to that evil the attention of others who might perhaps not have observed it; and in this way, if that bad quality really exists in the person whom they are so improperly criticizing, they distinctly increase it by strengthening the vibration which is its expression. If, as is usually the case, the depravity exists only in their own prurient imagination, and is not present in the person about whom they are gossiping, then they are doing the utmost in their power to create that evil quality in that person, and if there be any latent germ of it existing in their victim, their nefarious effort is only too likely to be successful.

Assuredly we may think helpfully of those whom we love; we may hold before them in thought a high ideal of themselves, and wish strongly that they may presently be enabled to attain it. If we know of certain defects or vices in a man's character we should never under any circumstances let our thoughts dwell upon them and intensify them; on the contrary we should formulate a strong thought of the contrary virtues, and then send out waves of that thought to the man who needs our help. The ordinary method is for one to say to another:

"O my dear, what a terrible thing it is that Mrs. So-and-So is so ill-tempered! Why, do you know, only yesterday she did this and that, and I have heard that she constantly, etc., etc.. Isn't it a terrible thing?

And this is repeated by each person to her thirty or forty dearest friends, and in a few hours several hundred people are pouring converging streams of thought, all about anger and irritability, upon the unfortunate victim. Is it any wonder that she presently justifies their expectations, and gives them yet another example of ill-temper over which they can gloat ?

A man wishing to help in such a case will be especially careful to avoid the idea of anger, but will think with all his force: " I wish Mrs. So-and-So were calm and serene; she has the possibility of such self-control within her; let me try frequently to send her a strong calm soothing influence, such as will help her to realize the Divine possibility within her". In the one case the thought is of anger, and in the other case it is of serenity; in both alike it will inevitably find its goal, and tend to reproduce itself in the mental and astral bodies of the person of whom the thought is made.

By all means let us think frequently and lovingly of our friends, but let us think of their good points, and try by concentrating our attention upon those to strengthen them and to help our, friends by their means; let our criticism be of that happy kind which grasps at a pearl as eagerly as the criticism of the average man pounces upon an imaginary flaw.

A man will often say that he cannot control his thought or his passion, that he has often tried to do so, but has constantly failed, and has therefore come to the conclusion that such effort is useless. This idea is wholly unscientific. If an evil quality or habit possesses a certain amount of strength within us, it is because in previous lives we have allowed that strength to accumulate — because we have not resisted it in the beginning, when it could easily have been repressed, but have permitted it to gather the momentum which makes it difficult now to deal with it.

We have in fact, made it very easy for ourselves to move along a certain line, and correspondingly difficult to move along another line — difficult, but not impossible. The amount of momentum or energy accumulated is necessarily a finite amount; even if we have devoted several lives entirely to storing up such energy (an unlikely supposition), still the time so occupied has been a limited time, and the results are necessarily finite. If we have now realized the mistake we made, and are setting ourselves to control that habit and to counteract that impetus, we shall find it necessary to put forth exactly as much strength in the opposite direction as we originally spent in setting up that momentum. Naturally we cannot instantly produce sufficient force entirely to counteract the work of many years, but every effort which we make will reduce the amount of force stored up. We ourselves as living souls can go on generating force indefinitely; we have an infinite store of strength on which to draw, and therefore it is absolutely certain that if we persevere we must eventually succeed. However often we may fail, each time something is withdrawn from that finite store of force, and it will be exhausted before we shall, so that our eventual success is simply a matter of mechanics.

You may have seen a railway porter, by steady and continuous pushing, set a big wagon or carriage in motion. Having brought it where he wishes, how does he stop it ? It is quite impossible for him, even by the exertion of his utmost strength, to check it instantaneously; so he puts himself in front of it and pushes vigorously against it, walking backwards as its advance forces him along, but never ceasing to exert his force against that advance. Thus by degrees he counterbalances the momentum which he has himself produced in it, and so at last wins his victory and brings it to rest. A good object-lesson in the neutralization of previous karma!

The knowledge of the use of these thought-currents makes it possible for us always to give assistance when we know of some case of sorrow or suffering. It very often happens that we are unable to do anything for the sufferer in the physical world; our physical presence may not be helpful to him; his physical brain may be closed to our suggestions by prejudice or by religious bigotry. But his astral and mental bodies are far more easily impressible than the physical, and it is always open to us to approach these by a wave of helpful thought or of affection and soothing feeling.

We must not forget that the law of cause and effect holds good just as certainly in finer matter as in denser, and that consequently the energy which we pour forth must reach its goal and must produce its effect. There can be no question that the image or the idea which we wish to put before a man for his comfort or his help will reach him; whether it will present itself clearly to his mind when it arrives, depends first upon the definiteness of outline which we have been able to give to it, and secondly upon his mental condition at the time. He may be so fully occupied with thoughts of his own trials and sufferings that there is little room for our idea to insert itself; but in that case our thought-form simply bides its time, and when at last his attention is diverted, or exhaustion forces him to suspend the activity of his own train of thought, assuredly ours will slip in and will do its errand of mercy. There are so many cases where the best will in the world can do nothing physically for a sufferer; but there is no conceivable case in which in either the mental or the astral world some relief cannot be given by steady concentrated loving thought.

The phenomena of mind-cure show how powerful thought may be even in the physical world, and since it acts so much more easily in astral and mental matter we may realize vividly how tremendous the power really is, if we will but exercise it. We should watch for an opportunity of being thus helpful; there is little doubt that plenty of cases will offer themselves. As we walk along the street, as we ride in a tram-car or a railway train, we may often see someone who is obviously suffering from depression or sadness; there is our opportunity, and we may immediately take advantage of it by trying to arouse and to help him. Let us try to send him strongly the feeling that in spite of his personal sorrows and troubles the sun still shines above all, and there is still much for which to be thankful, much that is good and beautiful in the world. Sometimes we may see the instant effect of our effort — we may actually watch the man brighten up under the influence of the thought which we have sent to him. We cannot always expect such immediate physical result; but if we understand the laws of nature we shall in every case be equally sure that some result is being produced.

It is often difficult for the man who is unaccustomed to these studies to believe that he is really affecting those at whom his thought is aimed; but experience in a great number of cases has shown us that anyone who makes a practice of such efforts will in time find evidence of his success accumulating until it is no longer possible for him to doubt. Each man should make it part of his life thus to try to help all whom he knows and loves, whether they be what is commonly called living or what is commonly called dead; for naturally the possession or the absence of the physical body makes no difference whatever to the action of forces which are leveled at the mental and astral bodies. By steady regular practice great good will be done, for we again strength by using it, and so while we are developing our own powers and ensuring our progress the world will be helped by our kindly efforts.

I remember seeing in an American book on mind-cure a passage which illustrates exceedingly well what should be the Theosophical attitude with regard to the duties and associations of daily life:

"Knead love into the bread you bake", it ran; "wrap strength and courage in the parcel which you tie for the woman with the weary face; hand trust and candour with the coin that you pay to the man with the suspicious eyes".

Quaint in expression, but lovely in its thought; truly the Theosophical concept that every connection is an opportunity, and that everyone whom we meet even casually is a person to be helped. Thus the student of the Good Law goes through life distributing blessings on all about him, doing good unobtrusively everywhere, though often the recipients of the blessing and the help may have no idea whence it comes. Never forget that in such benefactions every man can take his share, and every man ought to take his share; all who can think can send out kindly helpful thoughts, and no such thought has ever failed, or can ever fail while the laws of the universe hold. We may not always see the result, but the result is there, and we know not what fruit may spring from the tiny seed which we sow in passing along our path of Peace and Love.

The End

Otis
Ronda / David
Reod M.

Made in the USA
Columbia, SC
14 May 2021